A Drink Named Tequila

Text: José María Murià
Photography: Ricardo Sánchez

SECOND EDITION

EDITORIAL AGATA

Prologue

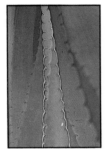 Besides being a strong alcoholic drink liked more by some than by others, tequila also holds a very special nationalistic significance for all Mexicans. Indeed, patriotic occasions are frequently celebrated with, among other things, toasts made with the drink seeking, in its effects, the enthusiasm which is sometimes lacking for the full, intense enjoyment of the event. It is not, of course, the only strong liquor produced in the Mexican Republic. Almost every region has its own: *sotol* in Chihuahua, *charanda* in Michoacán, *bacanora* in Sonora and *xtabentun* in Yucatán, etc.. However, tequila, originally and exclusively from Jalisco, has become a national symbol.

Today, it is sometimes mixed with a carbonated grapefruit or cola drink - a combination generally called a "changuirongo". Some time back, a combination of tequila, lime juice, crushed ice and a dash of cointreau, served in a champagne glass with salt around the rim, was baptised a "margarita". But the conventional way to drink tequila is straight, in small, cylindrical shot glasses, called "caballitos"[T1], or with a chaser of "sangrita" made from orange juice and spices, or simply with a bite of lime and coarse grains of salt to "inure" the throat, speeding the tequila on its downward path.

Nowadays, three kinds of tequila can be distinguished, according to the time that has elapsed from its manufacture to its appearance in the marketplace. Those who prefer the old forms drink "white", which usually has the highest proof, although there is also "joven abocado" which is smoother. Others ask for tequila that has "reposed" for more than two months in the so-called "pot-bellies" or casks made of dark or light-colored oak. Lastly, the most sophisticated class drinks the "añejo" ("aged") which has been waiting in the wings for between one and three years.

Similarly, it should be pointed out that the Mexican government's official standard of quality allows up to 49% of other sugars so that lower-cost tequilas can be produced, though many manufacturers prefer to display the legend "100% agave" on their labels, a status duly guaranteed by government supervision.

While the tendency these days is to seek to improve quality, there were times when some manufactures aspired only to sell larger quantities, colluding with certain ignorant or dishonest federal functionaries to the point where quality controls might have become even more lax. In the end, thanks in part to the fact that the area under tequila agave - which takes some ten years to mature - has grown so greatly, and because there is no danger of a shortfall in supply, at least in the near future, those favoring a purer, higher quality product prevailed.

Though not exempt from problems and conflicts, these are good times for tequila, whose fame is now poised to spread even further, but it was no easy task to reach this point. Besides the hope that this short text serves to encourage the tequila industry, it also constitutes an acknowledgment of the tenacity shown by a group of people –some involved in tequila manufacture, others simply defenders of all things Mexican– who were instrumental in steering the industry away from disaster. They include: Antonio Alvarez, Javier Solórzano, Carmen Aristegui, Felipe Remolina Roqueñí, Claudio Jiménez Vizcarra, Rogelio Luna, Francisco Néstor, Guillermo Romo and, finally, *don* Jaime Ruiz Llaguno, whose many virtues and dedication to the cause always make me remember him with great affection and reverence.

Once upon a time, there was a drink named tequila

In memory of Jaime Ruiz Llaguno, champion of fine tequila

Although the *maguey* [1] or *agave* is not unique to Mexico, it can accurately be said that in no other country in the world is it better integrated into the landscape and the people's emotions and way of life. Because of the many benefits it has brought, its image is interwoven with popular myths and legends, poetic forms of interpreting reality. These include the earliest allusions to its origin and nature.

In the Nahuatl culture, the maguey was a divine creation that represented Mayáhuel, a goddess who had four hundred breasts to feed her four hundred children. In this way, the early settlers of Anáhuac considered that the plant was an important nutrient, all the more so since Mayáhuel was married to Petácatl, who represented various plants that helped in the fermentation of *pulque* [2], thus meaning that the drink acquired more and stronger magical powers.

But only pregnant women, those medically prescribed it or the elderly could freely partake of pulque. We also know that it was given to warriors before they entered combat. In addition, pulque was used in cooked dishes and to enhance the nutritive value of bread. On the other hand, punishment for its unauthorized use could be as severe as death.

It is also worth adding that, from maguey leaves, fibers were obtained for the manufacture of cords and ropes as well as for the garments worn by the *macehuales*, or townsfolk. In the middle of the sixteenth century, the Franciscan, Toribio de Benavente, also known as *Motolinía* owing to the poverty of his attire, wrote the following:

> they pull, from those fleshy leaves of *metl*, thread to sew. They also make cords, ropes, thick ropes, saddle-girths and headstalls... clothing and footwear, that the Indians call *cactli*... they also make sandals like those of Andalucia, capes and cloaks.

The friar also said that the thorns themselves of the lanceshaped leaves were very useful as nails and needles, given that "they enter a wall and a plank", without overlooking their importance in ceremonial self-immolation. At the same time, he talked of the dry leaves being used to cover the roofs of houses or simply for lighting fires whose ashes, moreover, were "very good for lye".

The leaves of the maguey were also incorporated into the prehispanic pharmacy, since their hot juice cured "a stab-wound or a fresh gash" and snakebite. And, as if this wasn't enough, the original settlers in Mexico obtained a special kind of paper from the maguey, several examples of which, used for making various now-famous codices, still survive.

It was not in vain that the Carmelite, Juan de la Concepción, wrote as follows in his *Romance Histórico*:

From the maguey's twisted fibers
came many volumes of History
in which pages were the colors
characters forming from the knots.

«Three leagues to the northwest (of Guadalajara), is the flourishing town of Tequila, sorrounded by gardens and plantations of sugar and of a species of maguey, which here is smaller than that grown near Mexico City for the production of pulque, Mexico's favorite drink. Here there is no pulque. This smaller maguey plant is made to ferment and a stronger whiskey, called «chinguerite», obtained from its distillation...»

W.H. Hardy, 1825.

 Although many kinds of maguey look similar, Mexico has more than seventeen genera and species. Here, we will focus on tequila, a dry spirit obtained from a very special type of maguey, produced almost exclusively in a well-defined central district of what today is the state of Jalisco. Over time, it has passed down throats in many countries and been seen by thousands of pairs of eyes watching those "very Mexican" films which starred Jorge Negrete, Pedro Infante, Pedro Armendáriz, "Indio" Fernández and various others.

The word *tequila*, of Náhuatl origin, also has other meanings.[3] It is the name of a settlement, originally prehispanic, where almost twenty thousand people live today at 1,218 meters above sea level, some fifteen leagues, a little less than sixty kilometers, north-west of Guadalajara. Tequila is the main town of the municipality of the same name, which includes more than 170 smaller settlements.

Clearly visible nearby is a volcano, also called Tequila, which rises to a height of more than three thousand meters above sea level. In

PREVIOUS PAGE: Panoramic view of Tequila, Jalisco.

15

ancient times, it seems that it was highly active and the "nipple" at its peak, clearly distinguishing it from any other hill, is an enormous lava plug that was not completely expelled during its last eruption many hundreds of years ago.

Tequila is also the name of the local valley and, during the colonial period, of a corregidor's district in New Galicia[4], which by the end of the eighteenth century had become a district of the brand-new Intendancy of Guadalajara. In the following century, as independent life began, it became a province. In the beginning, it was only in this province where the alcoholic drink called tequila was produced, but with time and increased demand, the zone has widened. Lastly, reference should be made to the XII canton[5] of Jalisco, established in 1872, that was also named Tequila. The canton's seat was in the former town, now elevated to city status because of the growth brought about by the manufacture of the famous *mescal* in each of its 16 "taverns".

FOLLOWING PAGE: The Main Place of Tequila, Jalisco.

Of all the great rural businessmen, the
tequila producers were the last to move their
places of residence from the countryside,
perhaps because their activity called for
more care and personal attention.

The best soils are permeable loams, rich in elements derived from basalt, and also rich in iron whose oxidation gives them their caracteristic brown or reddish color.

 Although the indigenous people knew many different ways of using the maguey plant, one productive aspect, which would end up becoming the most important, awaited the arrival, accompanying Spanish domination, of the first Creoles and mestizos: the distillation of the must extracted from the heart of the maguey or agave.

In a slightly confused manner, Motolinía noted several things about the manufacture of a liquor made by cooking the maguey heart. He said he had heard it called locally *mexcalli*, "which the Spaniards say is of great substance and wholesome".

With the intention of favoring the importation and sale of produce from the major Iberian peninsular landowners, the Spanish Crown had prohibited the production of liquor in America, and brutally persecuted those who disobeyed. This, as well as to ensure - at least, so they said - that the Indians and mestizos would consume less, was why mescal was born and raised clandestinely. In turn, this explains why it took so long to leave clear proof of its existence and why today we know so little of its teething stages and first, tottering steps.

This is why, surely, neither Friar Alonso Ponce, who visited New

Galicia from 1586 to 1587, nor the diligent Alonso de la Mota y Escobar, Bishop of Guadalajara between 1589 and 1607, left any note whatever, in their extensive descriptions of all they had seen, about the manufacture of this "mescal wine". In fact, the first reliable information dates from 1621 when a priest, Lázaro de Arregui, writes that:

> The mescals are very similar to the maguey, and their root and the bases of their fleshy leaves are eaten grilled, and from them themselves, squeezing them thus grilled, they extract a must from which they get wine by distillation, clearer than water, much stronger than spirits and of that taste. And, though they claim many virtues for the mescal made, they commonly use it in such excess that they discredit the wine and even the plant.

But when the city of Guadalajara urgently needed more resources for public services, it was the Governor of New Galicia himself who decided in 1538 to regulate the production and trading of "mescal wine", ordering the creation of the corresponding state government store. This guaranteed the collecting of taxes and an unusual degree of quality control for everything that entered Guadalajara.

The local authority maintained that mescal was not harmful to health, as was said in Spain; rather, many medics certified its wholesomeness and suggested that its manufacture and sale be authorized. It was also said that not permitting Indians to consume it would cause them to flee to the mountains where they would partake of other brews that really were noxious.

However, the government store was soon closed. After its benefits were spent on constructing hot-water baths, criticized for being an unnecessary luxury in the face of other needs, its enemies succeeded in getting its license cancelled. But the idea was not forgotten and in 1673 it was ordered to re-open. Thanks to this source of income, Guadalajara's great scarcity of potable water could be corrected. As a result, the store's prestige increased and it survived until the post-independence liberal governments abolished all similar institutions, even if only for a ten-year parenthesis between 1785 and 1795.

Anyway, the store still faced sufficient opposition for Matías de la Mota Padilla to set out to defend it in 1742 in his book *Historia del Nuevo Reino de Galicia en la América Septentrional*. He pointed out that, unlike people from New Spain who normally drink pulque, those from New Galicia prefer mescal wine "for its greater strength". Mota went on to affirm that if removing the store would have ended "the use of mescal wine", revoking its license would have counted with his support, but he showed how that had not happened. On the contrary, its manufacture had tended to increase and its prohibition had favored the use of other drinks. In reality, what Mota was complaining about was that because there was not a government store in the seat of every administrative district, the government lost "many, and very excellent resources". And, reminding his readers how the income from the government store had served in 1735 to increase the amount of water that reached Guadalajara, he said "It is good that the profits of wine were converted into water". He further argued that if government stores were opened in every district seat, their resources could be allocated "to the construction of jails in the seats of jurisdiction, because there aren't any, from which it follows that the prisoners go on the run" or to repair the palace and the drawing rooms of the Royal Audience "since they are now almost fallen down".

In 1730, King Philip V had authorized that the revenues collected in the government store would be spent specifically on bringing water to the city and in making repairs to the Government Palace. The first was done in 1735; but the business of the palace took longer. In the first place, the construction of a new building was favored, then various projects were discussed and finally, almost thirty years later, the Crown approved the plans and the work began, albeit slowly.

In 1785, when the government store closed temporarily because the Viceroy, Matías de Gálvez, managed to get Charles III to definitively prohibit the manufacture and sale of alcoholic drinks in Mexico, the government in New Galicia lost this source of income and had to make several cuts in its plan to finish the second floor of the palace. In effect, about half of all the construction costs came from mescal. Ten years later, when the prohibition was lifted only on mescal, and the government store re-opened, the palace had already been finished.

Rhizome shoots are usually used in establishing plantations of tequila agave.

Agaves from which the flowering stalk or *quiote* has emerged, a sign of their maturity. From 10 to 14 years will elapse between planting and harvest, or last cutting.

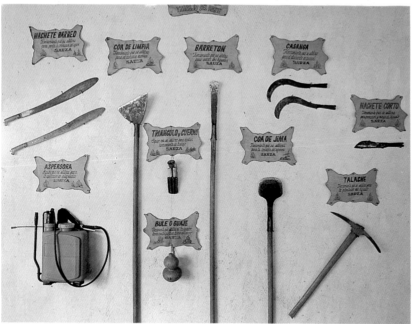

The jobs of tending the soil and the harvesting or *jima* of the agave require specialized tools for each task.

ABOVE:
The day laborer tending agaves carries, attached to his belt, a horn containing tallow, used to prevent getting blisters on his hands.

BELOW:
Exhibit showing various hand tools used in agave cultivation.

FOLLOWING PAGE:
gourd or *guaje* used by the worker as a flask.

The *jima* is the harvesting of the agave, consisting of cutting the plant and its leaves to leave an ovoid form which is the «head». The *jima* is carried out in the early hours of the morning and is a job that requires specially trained workers.

San Blas, officially founded in 1768, quickly became an active port, opening up the horizons of New Galicia and everything manufactured there. The bad news was that very little was being produced owing as much to the isolation New Galicia had experienced up to that point in time, as to its sparse population and the taxation conditions imposed on American industries in general by the peninsular metropolis. Thus, when conditions in New Galicia were right for trade, only raw materials and merchandise from other regions were available.

Practically the only article from New Galicia that it was possible to produce on a larger scale was "mescal wine", despite the scorn heaped on it in previous times. Of all the mescal wine produced in the region, that from the district of Tequila, thanks to the fame it had already gained and its proximity to San Blas, became Jalisco's foremost export product.

José Longinos Martínez, the famous naturalist who traveled through the Californias in 1792, wrote in his *Diario de la ciudad de México a San Blas* that, between Amatitán and Tequila, there were only plantations of mescal and that "many thousands" of barrels were "shipped each year".[6] Elsewhere, it was recalled, in 1846, how at an earlier time the department of Tequila had satisfied the demand in Sinaloa, Sonora and the Californias.

The "wine from this land" was similarly sought after in Mexico City on account of its superior consistency, even though other mescals, because they were made more locally, reached the capital of New Spain at a lower price. Even though many years were still to pass before it would be recognized scientifically that the agaves from Tequila were of a very distinct species, there were already palates that noted the difference.

It is also worth pointing out how one part of that rugged Sierra Madre, that long ago had been the principal obstacle to expansion northwards, had now become an important source of mineral wealth and a good market for Guadalajara and its region. This was the mining area of Bolaños which, as the eighteenth century drew to its close, required the delivery of many shipments of mescal wine.

In this period the district of Tequila fancied itself as one of the richest in the Intendancy of Guadalajara, with a church that "is surely the best one in all of it", as one, possibly exaggerated, account of the period intones. A rich harvest was reaped on the banks of the River Santiago: a "thousand loads" a year of coarse, brown sugar and almost a ton of refined sugar, from the sugar-cane sown to the south and south-west. But what proved to be even more profitable was the manufacture of mescal wine, which brought more than two thousand pesos a year into the local tax office.

Even though the prohibition against making mescal wine had been lifted in 1795, thus helping to considerably swell the coffers of the state of Jalisco, fear that the veto might return was always present. Perhaps for this reason, neither the producers and traders, nor even the local authorities, made any great fuss over the dividends obtained. As a result, information about the development of the mescal wine industry during the first decade of the nineteenth century is very scanty. Baron Alexander von Humboldt, for instance, erroneously claimed that mescal was made by "distilling pulque".

However, once Miguel Hidalgo enters Guadalajara at the end of 1810 and is defeated afterwards at Calderon Bridge, and the crisis in the peninsular government and the headaches caused by the insurgents ensure that neither Mexico nor Madrid will interfere very much in affairs in Guadalajara, more information about mescal wine comes to light showing that both its manufacture and its sales are increasing.

It is worth recalling here that, between 1812 and 1815, while the forces of José María Morelos dominated the southern coasts, the unloading of cargo coming from Asia had to be suspended in Acapulco and transferred to San Blas, which then became the only available port. As a consequence, trade in the region increased greatly. Fairs began in Tepic and the traditional fairs in San Juan de Los Lagos and Talpa acquired great splendor. This contributed to the consumption of mescal wine in the immediate region reaching previously unheard-of levels. The same happened with the mescal wine sent to Mexico City and that which, via San Blas, came to be savored by Filipinos, South Americans and Californians.

In precisely the same year that Morelos died —1815— San Blas registered its highest income from the handling of mescal wine and many other products. The next year, with the Acapulco route reopened, the figures for San Blas began to decline. Thus, when independence was consummated in 1821 the industry had greatly contracted, though the resulting freedom of internal and external trade helped prompt its recovery. By this time, the mescal wine from Tequila, its fame having grown enormously, had begun to be called "wine from this land" and begun to be highly solicited in the "taverns" that travelers, on passing through the Tequila district, encountered in both Amatitán and the district seat.

In 1824, the state of Xalisco - with "X" - elected Prisciliano Sánchez as its first governor. Sánchez, whose career was short but esteemed, was originally from, precisely, a mescal-producing region, Ahuacatlán, in what is now the state of Nayarit. He received decisive support from the leaders and landowners of the area.

The old method of production involved the «pineapples» being placed, after roasting, in a large, circular basin, known as a *tahona*, whose floor was covered with small, pointed stone slabs, around which a large mill wheel turned, drawn by one or two draught-animals.

ABOVE: chunk of cooked agave.
BELOW: a *tahona*, formerly known as a «Chilean mill».

Old
fermentation
tanks.

In the old method, the crushed agave and its juices were carried in buckets to the fermentation tanks, where a worker finished extracting the juices by moving all the material in the tank.

FOLLOWING PAGE:
Distillation is the process by which the products of fermentation are separated by heat and pressure into components rich in alcohol (tequila), and thick wines which are considered waste. In former times, distillation was performed in rustic stills like earthenware pots or in copper stills.

There was a time when barrels had the adventure
of traveling in carts from Tequila to beyond El Paso.

Towards 1880, tequila began to be bottled in «large flasks» and «demijohns» made of glass. This was an innovation, given that previously it had always been stored and moved in wooden barrels.

 We know that in the hacienda of La Cofradía de Animas, purchased in 1758 by José Antonio de Cuervo, a son, José María Guadalupe, was already making "wine from this soil" on a large scale by 1795.

This distillery —or *tavern*, as it was also called— was inherited by José María Guadalupe's daughter, who "married Vicente Albino Rojas in Tequila". She put him in complete charge of administering the factory, bequeathing it to him on her death. Vicente Rojas, already participating in the progressive individualism that would later characterize many of these industrialists, could not resist calling his own prosperous business after his father-in-law - "Cuervo's Tavern" - and soon he called it "La Rojeña". Later, the fashion spread and it became common for distilleries to be baptized with a feminine variant of the surname of their owner; Martinez: "La Martineña"; Guarro: "La Guarreña; Gallardo: "La Gallardeña"; Flores: "La Floreña"; Quintanar: "La Quintaneña", etcetera. It also became common to link the brand name with some positive quality, as in the case of the factory known as "The Ancient Cross", which Cenobio Sauza, its new owner, preferred to call "La Perseverancia" ("The Perseverance"), or when Jesús Flores changed the name of "La Floreña" to "La Constancia" ("The Certainty"). However, even today the old cross which had given its name to Sauza's distillery still points to the sky above Tequila from atop the distillery's very tall *chacuaco*.[7]

Three Europeans who wrote about their travels in Mexico dedicated a few lines to the department of Tequila, lines which, despite being of secondary importance, are nonetheless interesting.

They were the Italian adventurer J. C. Beltrami, the English trader W. H. Hardy and his fellow countryman T. Penny, from whose works it is worth quoting several paragraphs of special significance.

Beltrami, who must have passed through Tequila at the end of September 1823, wrote the following:

Although it is a beautiful town, it is surrounded by a region sterile to the eyes of a European; in Mexico, however, even poor land produces fruits and riches; the maguey and other indigenous plants lend to Tequila this prosperity denied by cereals... the maguey of Tequila offers a magnificent quality of spirits, the liquor called mescal wine.

Hardy, who passed through Tequila during the last days of December 1825 and the first days of 1826, affirmed that:

> Three leagues to the northwest (of Guadalajara), is the flourishing town of Tequila, surrounded by gardens and plantations of sugar and of a species of maguey, which here is smaller than that grown near Mexico City for the production of pulque, Mexico's favorite drink. Here there is no pulque. This smaller maguey plant is made to ferment and a stronger whiskey, called "chinguerite", obtained from its distillation....

It is curious to note how two authors who visited Tequila practically at the same time differ so greatly as far as the scenery is concerned. Beltrami, even though he came during the rainy season, considered it "sterile", coming as he did from a country which is excessively green, while Hardy, coming from the English fields and after passing through Tequila during the dry season, conceded that its surroundings were "gardens". But both agree that the principal characteristic of Tequila was the abundance of maguey. While the radical Italian was not especially impressed by either these agaves or their benefits, the Englishman whetted his lips in eager anticipation... After his stay in Jalisco, the other Englishman, T. Penny, showing less perspicacity or descriptive flair than Hardy, stated that "the wine... is extracted from maguey and constitutes the principal product of the western province". Indeed, Penny highlights something that has still not been sufficiently acknowledged - that during those early years of Mexican federalism Tequila's mescal wine was definitely the main industry in the state which had been the principal stronghold of opposition to centralism.

The educator Manuel López Cotilla recognized that Tequila was the "principal town in the district because of its trade in mescal wine, extracted by distillation from that plant which, as we have said, is a variation of maguey or American agave".[8] "Among the many wine factories it has", he continued, is one that stands out above all the others for its volume of production, which reaches "400 barrels a week".[9] He was referring, of course, to the already-mentioned "La Rojeña".

Moreover, López Cotilla said several things about Amatitán that belong in this account: "The principal occupation of its population, comprised of 1,300 inhabitants, is the distillation of mescal wine". He added that during the dry season work had to stop because of a lack of water. On the other hand, according to the same author, Tequila had "an abundance of water, fruit trees and vegetables".

Today, water still remains an extremely important factor, not only for the quality of the product but also for the volume of its production. It should be emphasized that the water must always be mineral-free.

In time, with greater pride in what was manufactured and a predictable desire to make the product stand out, the point was reached when "mescal wine from this soil" came to be called simply *tequila*.

The chronicle of Ernest Vigneaux, a French medic who passed through Tequila as a prisoner of war in 1854, besides affirming that "maguey is the most valuable gift that nature has given to Mexico" explains that "Tequila gives its name to mescal liquor, just like cognac gives its name to French liquors in general...."[10] Many years were still to pass before the name would become generally accepted in the top commercial and industrial circles, but it is evident that when Vigneaux was there, the name Tequila had been adopted to denominate the "mescal wine from this soil". Subsequently, documents employing the same meaning began to proliferate.

One of these was a little-disseminated manuscript by Manuel Payno, the famous author of *Los Bandidos de Río Frío*. The text in question is entitled *Memoria sobre el maguey mexicano y sus diversos productos*, and says:

> Pure mescal is one of the most highly regarded spirit liquors in the Mexican market. This liquor and the tequila that is made in the Department of Jalisco are commonly confused in odor and taste with Dutch gin....

Apart from the fact that Payno displays, by this comparison, only a superficial knowledge of gin - or poor taste discrimination - it is obvious that he had acquired the idea that what was called *tequila* and what was called *mescal* were not the same. Moreover, as if this was insufficient, in another part of the same text he reiterates that:

> Mescal wine is made on a large scale in Guadalajara and in San Luis Potosí. That from Guadalajara, generally known by the name tequila, is consumed throughout the country. That from San Luis Potosí is almost entirely exported to Guanajuato and Zacatecas and it is mostly miners who consume it.

José S. Anda affirms something of similar importance in *La Grana y el Mezcal*, published around 1870, when he states categorically that "tequila is made in Jalisco", although he declares his ignorance as to whether the origin of tequila is the same as that of mescal or "if, for both, the manufacture is identical".

Parallelling in time the more widespread use of the name "tequila", the liberalism of its producers resulted, logically, in support for the political group headed by Benito Juárez. This is well proven by the fact that it was to be exactly in Tequila where the Army of the West finally drove its enemies out of Jalisco, at the end of 1866. In fact, since 1858, the tequila manufacturers had given their support to Ramón Corona, the commander-in-chief of this army, when he had taken up arms to fight Manuel Lozada, at that time in the service of the important conservative businessmen.

Similarly, a prominent tequila manufacturer, Antonio Gómez Cuervo, was designated interim governor and military commander of the state of Jalisco by General Corona himself,[11] thus initiating the restoration of the republic. Moreover, later, at the end of 1867, Corona would arrange for his friend and former patron to be elected constitutional governor.

Predictably, Gómez Cuervo did not fail to respond to the interests of the tequila manufacturers. Barely four months into his governorship of Jalisco, he decreed a marked reduction in taxes on the product. Later, in response to a plague afflicting many agaves, he established an official prize for whoever discovered the cure. On the other hand, faced by the economic imperatives of the state, he did not hesitate to raise taxes on the textile industry and on various branches of commerce. Without any doubt, the development of the tequila industry owes much to the man who by hook or by crook, and with many mishaps, was governor of Jalisco for several years before he retired to private life in 1871.

On a different note, by 1873, there were 16 "taverns" in the town of Tequila. Given that its total population was then just 2,500 persons, the ratio was 156 inhabitants per factory.

So far as the manufacture of tequila in that period is concerned, from fields lacking tractors or other technical resources, the mescal "pine-apples" or heads were carried on the backs of mules or donkeys, six at a time at the most, to ovens where they were to be roasted. Previously, in the fields where the agave had been growing for ten years, the leaves of the mescal had been lopped off, a practice called the *jima*. After spending two or three days in the ovens, the pineapples were transferred to a large, circular basin, known as a *tahona*, whose floor was covered with small, pointed stone slabs, around which a large mill wheel turned, drawn by one or two draught-animals. This was known, from very early on, as the "Chilean mill". The must resulting from this process was deposited in large tanks, where it would remain for several days to ferment. Finally, it would pass to the stills for distillation. Afterwards, only the aging, the sale and the tasting remained.

Only after 1873 were conditions in the country suitable for industrial development. This made it possible to conceive of better techniques that would increase production and improve hygiene. It is said that in that same year, Cenobio Sauza made the first overland export of "three barrels and six jars" to the United States, destined for New Mexico.

Tequila had been sold for a time, by way of San Blas, to the gold prospectors in California even before the completion of the first coast-to-coast railroad across the United States in 1869 had tapped new drinking markets in the East and in Europe. But the casks from Sauza, that had the adventure of traveling by cart from Tequila to the other side of El

Paso del Norte, opened up the possibility that "the wine from this soil" could capture a very much larger market than the traditional one. By this means, 978 pesos worth of exports to the United States in 1873 became 2,740 in 1899. In addition, tequila sales began to European countries like Germany, Belgium, Spain, France and England, and to Guatemala and El Salvador which, between them, bought more than all the Europeans.

Back in Mexico at this time, Guadalajara and other, smaller cities, in both the state of Jalisco and its neighbor, began to experience rapid demographic growth; this greatly increased demand for the product. Consequently, steam-power soon made its debut in the manufacturing process, with the intention of speeding up the cooking of the "pineapples", previously done using only wood. At the same time, another type of mill, more efficient and less costly to maintain, began to extract a higher proportion of the juice from the fleshy leaves, and fermentation took place in tanks which were more hygienic, reducing the likelihood of waste.

Soon, booklets began to appear on how to improve production, about the product's benefits and its enormous possibilities, all inspired

Lázaro Pérez did not lose faith in the "promising future that mescal wine or tequila has, due to the Central Railroad, which in a very short time will provide us with rapid communication, not only to the principal cities in the Republic, but also overseas, where the afore-mentioned article will be widely consumed, especially when its good qualities are widely known and duly appreciated".

LA ANTIGUA CRUZ
1873

A good souvenir for the friends.

Old tequila labels and adds.

by a rhythm of transformation on which great hopes were placed. It was an age of *progress*, though this was interpreted only in terms of increased production and greater sales, without muchimportance being attached to the division of the spoils.

Of all the tequila-related bibliography of the final quarter of the last century, the most important work is *Estudio sobre el Maguey llamado Mezcal en el Estado de Jalisco*, written by Lázaro Pérez in 1887. Pérez, originally from Zapotlán el Grande[T2], was a famous chemist, prominent in Guadalajara on account of his teaching of the subject and his pharmacy, as well as for constructing the city's first meteorological observatory on the roof of his house.

In the first place, his pamphlet reveals how prevalent the use of the word *tequila* had already become to refer to the liquor of the agave in question, as well as the word's exclusive use for that liquor produced in the municipalities of Amatitán, Tequila, Magdalena, Hostotipaquillo, Ahualulco and Teuchitlán.

Despite this usage, a degree of reluctance lingered on. At the beginning of the twentieth century, some official statistics still insisted on including what all consumers knew simply as *tequila* in the general category of *mescal wine*. It is also worth recording here that as quickly as the Frenchification which characterized Mexico at the end of the century was being consolidated, the consumption of "wine from this soil" was becoming correspondingly little appreciated by those with the where-with-all to imbibe Spanish and French spirits.

However, Lázaro Pérez did not lose faith in the

promising future that mescal wine or tequila has, due to the Central Railroad, which in a very short time will provide us with rapid communication, not only to the principal cities in the Republic, but also overseas, where the afore-mentioned article will be widely consumed, especially when its good qualities are widely known and duly appreciated.

He considered it necessary, nevertheless, that the stubborn manufacturers abandon their antique manufacturing systems, with which the resulting product was "more empyreuma-charged",[T3] in favor of a system "based on scientific principles", which would allow them to obtain "higher purity and more abundance". In order that his exhortation would be more effective, he cited as examples the success achieved by those who had already gone down this road: Jesús Flores in Tequila and Luis Labastida in Teuchitlán. On the other hand, he announced that:

in a modern-style distillation factory, considerable sums must be spent [but he added that] whoever has such sums available must not hesitate in giving them useful and gainful employment, in the certainty that, just from the additional profits produced by that factory, not many years will pass before the money which has been invested will be recouped.

Pérez also wrote of the characteristics of agave, of its enemies, of the best form of planting it, of making tequila, of its physical and chemical properties and of its final composition. A highly significant moment in his account comes when he mentions what the benefits of the product are, provided that, "understand this well", it is used appropriately and in due moderation. It is convenient to let Pérez himself explain the "virtues of this drink that have been confirmed by experience":

It revives the natural appetite for meals in persons who for some reason have lost it; improves the digestive process; tones gastric functions; has a positive effect in those illnesses in which debility plays the main part and in those dispepsias which are often resistant to all known Therapeutic agents; it speeds up the healing of shallow wounds, at the first attempt, when they are washed and dressed with it; it reduces pain and prevents the general inflammation resulting from sprains when applied in fomentations; it invigorates bodily functions weakened by age; it slakes the thirst caused by insolation, a property taken advantage of by many walkers, thereby avoiding illnesses, sometimes fatal, brought about when they satisfy an imperative necessity by using natural water; it greatly extenuates the effects produced on the body on certain occasions by a sudden drop in ambient temperature; it calms the unpleasant feeling of hunger, for many hours, being a "breathing" food; it restores the strength spent from working too much; it heightens intelligence, chases boredom away, and produces agreeable illusions....

Despite the fact that the uses of this plant, generally referred to as maguey, had been known, one way or another, for hundreds of years, knowledge of its peculiarities and, above all, of how to distinguish its many variants, had advanced but little.

It was only as the eighteenth century drew to a close that the illustrious Swedish naturalist Carl von Linné took the first steps in this direction, steps from which the name Agave, meaning "magnificent and admirable", emerged. The maguey which grew in this country first became known as Mexican agave at the beginning of the nineteenth century, using the definition of a Frenchman, Jean Baptiste de Lamarck.

It seems, according to León Diguet, a French chemist who was in Jalisco in 1898, that a botanist whose surname was Weber was the first to typify the tequila agave and establish, by means of an article published in a 1902 *Museum Bulletin*, the differences between it and its close relatives of the same genus. Likewise, he proposed that its scientific name be *Agave tequilana*, hence the name that soon came to be used for its designation was *Agave tequilana Weber*. Later *azul* ("blue") was added, given that its tendency towards this color constitutes the most obvious distinguishing characteristic when the plant is healthy.

Notwithstanding the disdain that elegant folk felt for tequila, they did not fail to recognize either its importance or that of the industry. Nor did they fail to take advantage of the revenues it contributed to the state's economy. On the first Saturday in May 1880, for example, the second exhibition of the famous society called "The Productive Classes" was inaugurated; practically all the manufacturers in the region attended. The "mescal wine" of Jesús Flores, "owner of one of the richest factories in Tequila", was predominant in this exhibition. About 660,000 liters of his product had already been sold between July 1879 and the following June, just in the city of Guadalajara.

According to one witness,[12] Flores presented his tequila in "large flasks" and "big bottles". This was an innovation, since until this time it had always been stored and transported in wooden barrels. However, more than thirty years were still to pass before this type of container became widespread. On the other hand, it was also said that the "products of Mr. Flores' factory have a good reputation at home and abroad", which shows that exports were already common.

Afterwards, in 1888, Joaquín Rom Vivar wrote that tequila wine was one of the products whose sales had increased most during recent years and that everything indicated that this trend would continue. A teacher in the Teachers' College[13] who, in 1897, published the second edition of a small *Geografía Particular del Estado de Jalisco* said that "on average" 3,400 barrels of "mescal wine" were produced annually, and later, in a fifth edition of the same work, published in 1914, asserted that "on average" it now exceeded 70,000. This growth had not involved the opening of many more factories, but rather the expansion of those already in existence. The sixteen industrial plants registered in Tequila in 1873 had increased to only eighteen by 1899.

Although it had now started along the right path, the tequila business was still not yet a true industry, given that it remained dominated by the kind of businessman who was not concerned one iota about seeking new markets or improving production techniques. But times were changing; precisely at the end of the nineteenth century came the first really important steps in search of greater international recognition and consumption. That is why the traveling Italian, Adolfo Dollero, referred to tequila as "the famous industrial product that has now crossed the Ocean".[14]

Evidence of this is on display in any of the hundred-year-old factories: the various diplomas and trophies won in fairs and exhibitions, both national and overseas, that were then the best means managers had available for exchanging products and winning markets. During the first thirty years of this century, the commercial organizations arranging these events were not stingy in awarding the most stunning trophies, diplomas, medals and cups possible, so that they might be shown off on brand labels and ostentatiously displayed in the offices of the favored company. Today, on the other hand, they are seldom shown even privately in some timid, wary fit of nostalgia. It is worth adding that the number of prizes awarded fell sharply after the Second World War.

Of all the great rural businessmen, the tequila producers were the last to move their places of residence from the countryside. As the twentieth century began, it is well known that practically all the hacienda owners had relegated their ancestral residences to the role of summer homes or for occasional visits, given that now their greatest desire was to figure prominently in the loftiest circles of society in Mexico's provincial capitals, the capital of the Republic, or even in Paris or some other flashy European city.

But the tequila producers, because their activity called for more care and personal attention, continued to live on their farms or in the nearby towns. It was not until after the end of the Mexican Revolution and the later Cristeros War, and of the resulting insecurity caused by the toing and froing of different opposing groups, that they emigrated to Guadalajara. They were also driven out by the crisis in the industry caused by the upheavals as well as by their desire to seek, from Guadalajara, new ways of expansion.

They soon became accustomed to the advantages of life in the city, from where it was now possible for them to continue managing their businesses. The Pacific Railroad, which greatly increased the possibilities of exporting to the United States, had been finished in 1927, and shortly afterwards, just before 1940, the use of motor vehicles was becoming more common enabling them to travel to or from Tequila in under an hour on a well paved road.

Similarly, the empirical training that the tequila producers had previously received was complemented by their offspring attending university. They soon introduced new knowledge and objectives to the old family industry. At the same time, it also became possible to contract graduate personnel for tasks that now required better training.

Agave fields, with their highly characteristic appearance, are now scattered through a large belt of central Jalisco's landscape. In addition, the industrialization of tequila involves, directly or indirectly, some 300,000 people.

The transporting of «pineapples» to the oven.

Some tequila manufacturers crush the agave pineapples before putting them in the oven.

Reposada («reposed») tequila is left for at least two months in wooden containers made of oak.

The stills used for distillation are copper or stainless steel.

ABOVE AND BELOW:
Quality control and
bottling.

FOLLOWING PAGE:
Aged, *añejo* tequila is
a product that must
mature for at least a
year in oak barrels.

ABOVE:
Within each company are groups of formal or informal tasters. Sometimes these are comprised of members of the traditional tequila-producing family; in others, groups of tasters from within the same company have been specially trained.

BELOW:
Annual production of tequila exceeds 50 million liters, half of which leaves the country.

 An important step for the greatly increased commercialization of tequila and, above all, for this to be achieved with greater ease was, without doubt, the use of glass bottles after the tequila had finished aging. The first bottles were brought from Germany but viewed with suspicion by a fraternity that was now sufficiently proud of tradition that it would not undertake change without the absolute certainty of its benefits. But the advantages were soon recognized and tequila could reach the palates that wanted it, with greatly improved hygiene. In this respect an outstanding part was played by the glass factory founded in Monterrey in 1906, from which the necessary quantity of bottles could be obtained.

Tequila thus acquired a more convenient presentation, one with a certain medicinal air. This coincided with a widespread epidemic which broke out in Zacatecas and San Luis Potosí, in about 1918, of a kind of influenza called "Spanish flu". To fight it, doctors proceeded to prescribe a treatment based on tequila, lime and salt which, even if it was not really a cure, did serve to cheer up sick patients to some degree, as well as manufacturers.

Thanks also to the bottles, during the twenties, large quantities of tequila began to be sent on a regular basis to the bubbling petroleum waters off Tamaulipas. In the succeeding decade, the oil bonanza declined because of competition from new wells in the Middle East, and the tequila market contracted, just as the final stage of agrarian reform complicated the situation still further. However, the start of the second Great War brought an international demand for tequila that its producers had never dreamt of. This demand was propelled by the publicity of a Mexican movie-making industry that for more than a decade had held strong appeal for all of America and a good part of Europe. But the greatest benefits of this wartime boom came neither to the tequila region nor to the tequila manufacturers. On the contrary, the latter were to suffer the disagreeable consequences of the abuses that would be committed.

Those who really took advantage of the situation were those who, by means of various systematic subterfuges, managed to acquire the bottles in advance and control the railroad cargo wagons. The tequila producers were inevitably forced to sell their production to them, remaining one step removed from the huge profits of an export trade which, to add insult to injury, had been given a head start and took very few sanitary measures.

As was to be expected, when the armistice was signed and liquor production recovered in the countries affected by the war, tequila exports fell to rock bottom. In 1940, 21,621 liters had been exported. This figure rose dizzily to almost 4,500,000 in 1944 - almost the same as 1970 exports - while, by 1948, less than 8,800 liters left the country.

It was then that the first commercial glass factory was founded in Guadalajara and, restarting the fight to acquire reputation and lost markets, important technical and sanitary improvements were made, without sacrificing quality. Besides this, several brands, by reducing their strength,[15] became accessible to more delicate throats.

Likewise, a precise legal standard was sought for the strict control of quality, in order to avoid the risk that when higher levels of production and sale were reached another disaster might occur. Since Guadalajara was already the economic center of the tequila industry, it was this city that saw the creation of the institutions needed to promote the industry and protect it from counterfeit products, which were damaging as much for the drink's prestige as for the health of those unwary enough to drink them.

The first, timid attempts by a large group of manufacturers in this direction were Productores de Tequila S.A., born in 1933, and its heir, Tequila S.A., which came into the world a couple of years later. Had either worked out opportunely, much discontent would have been spared, but both failed in their attempt to be "the only producer of tequila made in the state of Jalisco". Suffice it to say that the lack of control caused by the surprisingly large demand that occurred post-1939 made it impossible to avoid the very damaging, previously-mentioned piracy.

In 1955 Tequila S.A. became the Productores de Tequila de Jalisco, S.A. de C.V., which immediately set about registering a trade mark "to protect and distinguish the diverse kinds of alcoholic liquors made by its members in their various factories". This was finally achieved in 1958.

In October of that same year, given that piracy such as that suffered by tequila also afflicted products from other countries, representatives of many governments met in Lisbon, under the aegis of the Union for the Protection of Industrial Property, founded in Paris in 1883. The meeting's purpose was to establish official standards protecting "the denomination of origin claims of products in the signatory states".

In 1959, inspired by the Lisbon Accord, the Regional Chamber of the Tequila Industry, officially recognized by the Industrial and Trade Secretariat, was also founded in Guadalajara. This immediately brought all the manufacturers together. Their desire to oversee good production practices prompted the formation, in 1994, of a Tequila Regulatory Council, with authority over all the product's manufacturing and entrusted with the task of combatting piracy at home and abroad.

With the increase in demand, other regions with similar natural conditions also began to cultivate blue agave. In some cases, like that of Tamaulipas, their failure was resounding, but others proved very successful. Such was the case of the Los Altos region of Jalisco, whose dabbling dated from the first years of this century. After 1932, this gave rise to an ever-growing number of distilleries there which, like those in the neighborhood of Tequila, have achieved great prestige and a very considerable production, especially during the past decade.

Of thirty-five distilleries that were in Jalisco in 1972, for example, nineteen were inside what was once the department of Tequila: fourteen in the municipality of the same name, two in the municipality of Amatitán and three in El Arenal, where many of the barrels used for storage are also manufactured. But the remaining sixteen are outside this area: ten are located in the Los Altos region, in Atotonilco el Alto, Tepatitlán and Arandas, and the others are in the municipalities of Zapopan, Tala, Acatlán de Juárez, Guadalajara and Zapotlanejo.

Water, indispensable for the making of the liquor, can be harmful to the agave if it is not in measured amounts. For this reason, it is necessary to grow it where both surface and subsurface drainage are good, which is why so many hillsides in Jalisco now bristle with mescal plants.

The ideal location is a "semiarid" climate with temperatures which vary little from an annual average of about 20° Centigrade, rainfall of around 1000 millimeters a year, an altitude of about 1,500 meters above sea level and where the sky is cloudy between 65 and 100 days a year. The best soils are permeable loams, rich in elements derived from basalt, and also rich in iron whose oxidation gives them their characteristic brown or reddish color.

Notwithstanding international accords and agreements stating that our drink can only be legitimately manufactured in one particular region of Mexico, the sad fact is that it is falsified with impunity in various countries, with terrible results in terms of quality.

Be that as it may, agave fields, with their highly characteristic appearance, are now scattered through a large belt of central Jalisco's landscape. In addition, the industrialization of tequila involves, directly or indirectly, some 300,000 people, all proud to participate in creating a product so strongly woven into the fabric of life of Mexico's western region. Exporting the majority of production to the four corners of the globe, they take pleasure each year in supplying the market with more than 100,000,000 liters of this drink which, when taken in moderation, is so full of good qualities.

Though not exempt from problems and conflicts, these are good times for tequila, whose fame is now poised to spread even further.

FOLLOWING PAGE:
It should be pointed out that the Mexican government's official standard of quality allows up to 49% of other sugars so that lower-cost tequilas can be produced, though many manufacturers prefer to display the legend "100% agave" on their labels, a status duly guaranteed by government supervision, in this case both strict and efficient.

Notes

1. Maguey is a word that comes from the West Indies. It is *metl* in Náhuatl, *tocamba* in Purépecha and *quada* in Otomi.

2. Pulque is primarily obtained in central Mexico, from a large, broad-leafed maguey. The heart is pressed and the juice left to ferment. It was employed as a ritual intoxicant but also used for food.

3. Etymologically, there are two versions of its meaning. The most viable is "place of wild grasses" but some say it means "place where one cuts" or "place where one works".

4. This is what the west of Mexico was officially called throughout almost all the time of Spanish domination, until 1786.

5. A political division that existed in Jalisco during the last century. There were eight when the first constitution of the free and sovereign state of Xalisco was proclaimed in 1824, and twelve at the end of the nineteenth century.

6. José Longinos Martínez. *Diario de la ciudad de México a San Blas.*

7. Chimney.

8. Manuel López Cotilla. *Noticias Geográficas y Estadísticas del Departamento de Jalisco.* 1841.

9. One barrel is approximately equivalent to 66 liters.

10. Ernest Vigneaux. *Souvenirs d'un prisonnier de guerre au Mexique.*

11. Ramón Corona Madrigal was then the General-in-Chief of the Army of the West, with extraordinary powers granted by President Benito Juárez.

12. Mariano Bárcenas. *Descripción de Guadalajara en 1880.*

13. José M. Nájar Herrera.

14. Adolfo Dollero. *México al Día. (Impresiones y notas de viaje).* Paris/ Mexico. Lib. de la Vda. de C. Bouret. 1911, p. 132.

15. Some brands are less than 40 degrees proof, though old-style drinkers prefer stronger brands.

16 Between 7 and 32 degrees Centigrade.

Translator's notes:

T1. Literally "little horses", colloquially used for "little beast" or "little brute".

T2. Jalisco's second city, now known as Ciudád Guzmán.

T3. Not commonly used in English, empyreuma is the burned smell and acrid taste that come when vegetables or animal substances are burned.

The second edition of *A Drink Named Tequila* was printed and bound in November 1997 by Editorial Agata. 1st edition, November 1996. **Text: D.R.** © **José María Murià, 1996. Photography: D.R.** © **Ricardo Sánchez**, 1996 (the photographs which appear in this book form part of a project undertaken with the assistance of the Jalisco State Fund of Culture and Arts; the photographer expresses his sincere appreciation to the following for their invaluable assistance: Benjamín García, of Tequila Cuervo; Luis E. Margain, of Tequila Herradura; Víctor R. Galindo, of Tequila Sauza; Lucrecia González, of Tequila Siete Leguas and Felipe Camarena, of Tequila Tapatío). The publisher wishes to acknowledge Fototek for the use of a photograph of "La Perseverancia", a mural painting by Gabriel Flores. **Translation from the Spanish: Tony Burton. This edition: D.R.** © **Agata Editores, S.A. de C.V., 1997**, calle Pino Suárez núm. 169, Guadalajara, Jalisco, México. **Graphic design: Rodolfo Sánchez Gómez.**

ISBN 970-657-000-4 (Spanish) / ISBN 970-657-004-7 (English) / ISBN 968-7310-80-4 (French) / ISBN 968-7310-81-2 (German)